TAIZÉ
A Meaning to Life

G-4755

Olivier Clément

TAIZÉ
A Meaning to Life

GIA Publications, Inc.
Chicago

ISBN: 1-57999-007-X

CONTENTS

5: An Inrush of Light, Peace and Love

6: From Anguish to Trust

7: Love Offered to All

INTRODUCTION

As a young man, when I was beginning the tough process of learning what life is, as many of my readers are doing now, I lived in a radically atheistic environment. I had not been baptized as a child; but I found myself with many questions, searching amidst anguish and wonder.

It was amazing to find myself living, breathing and walking. And walking, when you are young, is almost dancing: quite unconsciously, it expresses an abundance of life! But I was also agonized by the nothingness in which it seemed that everything was going to be engulfed. I had asked my father about death, and he had replied: "Death is nothingness. But still," he added, "we must try to live with uprightness and integrity." I had doubts whether this was a coherent conclusion: there must have been something else that drove him to speak this way, but it seemed he did not have the words to express it.

Nothingness. I scrutinized the idea: nothing. So everything was going to end in nothing. And so everything was not worth very much now. And to add to the absurdity of this there was the war going on, and there were the totalitarian regimes. Nevertheless, it seemed to me that a total absence of meaning left too many questions unanswered. For humankind is not a creature of nothingness: we are forged out of "whys." Even today, I still keep on asking "why" about things, which sometimes annoys my wife, who imagines I am asking her! But in reality, "whys" are actually a sort of prayer....

Why is there all this beauty when the almond trees flower? A few flowers would be enough, a few small machines well designed for plant reproduction. But there is this gratuitous profusion, this immense light in the blue. And this earth, where we die, seems to open onto light.

Matter is something that cannot be grasped; it is a mathematical abstraction. But why, then, are there shapes sculpted into it? What are these invisible structures which take form within it and which never stop turning the processes of disintegration and chaos into rich and complex integrations?

And what is a face—something that may be heavy and brutal, but which can suddenly light up with a twinkling of the eyes, with a smile?

And why do we experience love, which is actually something much more than love, I mean much more than desire—something like the revelation of a presence? A character in a play I had read said: "To love someone is to say to them: you are not going to die." I experienced something like this on one occasion during the war. I was being questioned, and after a fairly harsh interrogation, the young German officer at last really saw my face: the thin face of an adolescent darkened by hunger. And his eyes woke up, he smiled, gave me back my identity card which he knew was false, and let me go....

And finally, why do we have this idea of death? It is an idea that animals do not have; they only have a quick fear at the last moment. But for us, why does death so often seem something contrary to nature? And since this is so, what then is our true nature? At that time in France, when someone died they died at home, and it was the custom to keep watch over the body. On one occasion, I had to keep watch over a body, and at times during that night the face expressed an unexpected peace, as if it was sealed by a beauty coming from elsewhere.

Life was sometimes so intense that all these questions seemed empty. But still.... I was walking one evening along the sea shore, and as the sun set it traced a long silver path on the waves. And I became filled with sadness: was all this splendor nothing but the mask of the void? The beauty of the world does not console us: it needs to be consoled.

Yes, there were Christians, and I sometimes came across them. They were just like everyone else. They did not seem to love life; in fact, more often than not, they seemed to be afraid of it. What they had was "morality," something which at times only made them mean. And furthermore, I wanted to know why God had only spoken long ago, in words collected in a huge book that had been closed for nearly two thousand years; why did he not speak any more today? And then there was this business of hell, as if God was more spiteful and cruel than human beings.... And what about evil, if God knew everything and could do everything, sitting comfortably in his eternity?

Nevertheless, I began little by little to sense a meaning in things. I was fascinated by the history of civilizations. And I discovered that most of them had been built up around a core of fire, something which I did not know how to name. I discovered that there had been, and that surely there still were, sages and poets, mystics who knew how to keep silence and how to speak; there were creators of life, justice and beauty. And through them God was still speaking, just as he had spoken to me before through the sunlit almond tree. So I came to understand that there were not only questions, but that there were answers too. These answers seemed to come from "elsewhere," from the dimension that I had already sensed in the vividness of things and in the mystery of people's faces. In fact, they were revelations. They were varied, they were sometimes apparently contradictory, but what did it matter! The important thing was to have found that the world was penetrated by an immense Breath of life, and that death did not have the last word.

Little by little, these revelations came together in a way that seemed to center around a face and also around a message: the face and the word of Christ. Now, Christ is a person; he is a secret companion who gently puts his hand on our shoulder in moments of loneliness and despair. He is a person, but a person without limits; a person who had passed through death and was stronger than death. He is the "fullness of humanity," gathering up in himself the whole human race and all creation as far as the furthest stars. He is a person, but one who opens onto what could be called an abyss of personhood, an abyss from which liberation and love came through him to all of us, or an abyss of "father-hood"— a term that expresses both distance and affection. All of us have known, or else we are looking for, someone like this. It may be our physical father, but it is more often a spiritual father —someone whose presence could be both attentive and discreet, not too close but yet affectionate. This idea is pathetic if everything is doomed to die. But it is a profound symbol if, at the core of things, at the heart of the world, there really does exist this abyss of liberating love.

The message of the heart of Asia, of India, of Buddhism said to me: "The only thing that counts is this abyss. It does not have a face: it is an ocean of bliss in which everything is dissolved. As for us, we are only dolls made of salt, and our destiny is to melt into it." On the other hand, the message of Europe was this: "The existence of every human being is individual and unique; but all of us are islands in a different ocean, the ocean of solitude." Did I then have to choose between them and decide either for a unity that meant fusion or else for a differentiation with no real contact? Either we do not exist, myself and the other, or else we are ultimately apart.

So it was at this point that I felt a resonance with the words of Jesus in the Gospel of John: "I and the Father are one." And then, talking about human beings, he said later on: "May they be one as we are one". And then I read a book by a great Russian émigré theologian who spoke about the unimaginable but adorable coming together in God (and therefore also in humanity, "made in God's image") of absolute unity and absolute diversity. They were both there together, the Hindu sense of unity and the European sense of difference! And this was called Communion, and it was called the Trinity, the fulness and the source of love.

And then this God who was "Love without limits" (in the words of "a monk of the Eastern Church") was not a distant sort of God, living in an overpowering eternity. No, he was a God who takes risks, a God who becomes incarnate, and in the end a God who is crucified. This God is not the author of evil; on the contrary, he is wounded by evil, crucified by evil. Yes, he is crucified without ceasing on the horrors of the world, yet ceaselessly rising from the dead and opening up unexpected ways of resurrection for us. He does not impose anything—what kind of love could impose anything, or even impose itself?—but acts like a wave of light and peace, or like a Life in which death changes its direction and gets wiped out as soon as the heart of a man or woman, with the "yes" of Mary, is freely opened to him. This is a God who is incarnate, crucified, and risen, and whose Spirit opens an infinite space for our newly released freedom, which becomes responsible and creative. This is also a God who deepens and enlarges our earthly joys, even the humblest ones, and makes them into something eternal: he is the one who changed the water of ordinariness into the wine of wild love at the wedding at Cana, who made the crowd sit down "on the green grass", so rare in Palestine, before sharing out food that would not run out, and who lit a fire of burning coals beside the lake to grill some fish and offer it to his friends. This is a God who is infinitely close to us, deeper within us than we are ourselves, so that however deep our despair may be, he is there, deeper still, standing between us and the void. This is a God who does not create hell—that is something we can manage very well by ourselves!—but who never stops descending into hell to release us; and all the great mystics, uniting themselves to him, have never stopped "pouring out their heart's blood" so that everyone may be saved.

In all my thinking and all my searching, I could not avoid coming across Taizé. I was deeply moved by the brief and luminous texts of Brother Roger, some of which are collected into books that you would like to carry about with you, maybe like carrying a gourd of fresh water in the desert. Yes, I was almost jealous of these texts, because they expressed what I felt, and what I made a poor attempt to live out; but they expressed it with a crystalline simplicity that I could never reach. "This is the way to talk to young people," I thought, "but as for myself, I only manage to speak to theologians!" What fervor fills Brother Roger's words about "Jesus, the Christ"—that is, the Messiah, the Envoy, the one through whom God is constantly coming towards us! He talks of a God who never punishes, but saves, and who sweeps through us with light. And if the warm clarity of this light makes us condemn ourselves, straight away we sense that "the cross is the condemnation of condemnation," as the Church Fathers say.

Soon I discovered not only the thinking but the peaceful creative strength of Brother Roger and his companions, which is like a magnetism that draws thousands upon thousands of young people to Taizé each year. It is a flood that is always new, making Taizé into an incredible meeting place where a spiritual dimension of Europe is being built up. Brother Roger speaks to these young people, always briefly and with utter simplicity; his words have, you could say, a love that seems almost helpless. In a world where many promises are made, but where scoffing at them is the rule, Taizé is a place with a totally different feeling. Guardians of orthodoxy, do not worry! Taizé is not trying to capture anyone; it does not claim to be a church. It wants only to be a sign of the Church and a way into it, in the perspective of reconciliation. People are "awakened" at Taizé: to silence, to prayer, and to friendship. And by means of friendship they discover that Christianity is a real possibility. Then they go back to their own countries with an irrepressible zest for this awakening and for this friendship.

At this point, I need to say something not only about the crowds of young people who keep coming to Taizé, but also about the monastic community that has gathered around Brother Roger and without which nothing else here would exist. It all began at a time during the Second World War when many people were thrown back on the basic essentials. In the face of horror and of death, it was not possible for them to lie to themselves any more. And it was not possible for them, as they tried to live the Christian life, to remain divided. Taizé was founded in the same spirit as the ecumenism of the prison camps: an ecumenism put into practice as mutual service and as a hope that could not be separated from prayer and love.

The community grew, without premeditation, like a living organism, or like yeast gradually being worked into the dough of history. It was like a witness to an alternative history, the history of the upside-down world expressed in the beatitudes, the history of the poor and the neglected who, nevertheless, are the ones who stop the Herods and the Pilates of the world from destroying humanity. At Taizé there is a group of young men who are full of life: they are liberating themselves from the idolatries of the world in order to be available for God and for all these young people to whom they offer an unselfish friendship. And so they are "separate from all and united to all," to use a phrase from one of the Egyptian monks of the end of the fourth century—a monk who was particularly attentive and clear-sighted.

These brothers, monks who keep their hands empty so as to be filled by God alone, belong to various Christian denominations. They have the sense that in reality there is only one Church, and that this One Church is the secret bedrock of all the churches, and that therefore unity is not something to be built but something to be discovered. They are looking for the re-emergence of the undivided Church which is still, in spite of all kinds of tensions and problems about identity, the crucial phenomenon of our time.

At Taizé, people from different and sometimes opposing denominations, cultures, races, and languages pray and work together. Yes, it is really possible; Christ destroys every separating wall. This historical and geographical variety becomes unimportant beside the variety of personal gifts. The community is a beehive of activity. Some brothers are creators of beauty: they paint pictures or icons, or they produce wonderful pottery which can ennoble everyday life. Others make translations and print important works from the Christian tradition. Languages are also studied, in response to the international calling of the community. It is a small but deeply experienced foretaste of the reconciled and transfigured humanity towards which history is painfully groping; and in this process of history, the Spirit is always at work, undermining whatever is impenetrable yet illuminating the creations of art, science and spirituality.

Young people today are tired of talk and tired of scoffing: they want authenticity. It is no use talking to them about communion if we cannot show them a place where communion is being worked out—"come and see." At such a place people are welcomed as they are without being judged; no one is asked for their doctrinal passport; but nevertheless no secret is made of the fact that everyone is gathered around Christ, and that with him—"I am the way," he said—a way forward begins for those who want it. At Taizé, you can find a kind of Christianity that I like to call "post-ideological."

God, said one of the Church Fathers, is "always to be sought for", but at the same time he never stops coming towards us and giving himself. That is to say, God is the Hidden One, the Secret and he is also Love; and so in the light of Christ we can come to see other people too as secret and as love.

At Taizé, people sing together, using phrases that are short but full of meaning and that are tirelessly repeated. The words of these songs come from the East and from the West, from North and South; they are easy to scan and to sing in different languages. On Friday there is the cross, and on Saturday night and Sunday morning there is the resurrection; every day you see Brother Roger taking children by the hand to teach them the gestures of prayer. Between the times of prayer, the brothers give commentaries on the Gospel. And it is possible to confide in them individually. They are not gurus but people who are searching like everyone else, only a bit further along the way. And then there is the extraordinary silence, which thousands of people allow to penetrate them....

This book is composed of a series of reflections based on dialogues that I have had at Taizé at different times. It is marked by the searching of the brothers and by questions of the young people whom they welcome. In these reflections I have wanted to go to the essentials without claiming to be exhaustive. The reason this book has been produced, and I would like to insist on this to finish with, is because for a long time I have felt a deep closeness between my own personal search and that of Taizé. Taizé has become one of my spiritual homes. I am Orthodox, and at Taizé I recognize the vocation of Orthodoxy when it goes beyond its historical limitations and bears witness to the original and the ultimate. It is like recognizing something shared, or like hearing an appeal.

It is an immense joy for me to see so many young Orthodox Christians from eastern and south-eastern Europe coming to Taizé by the bus-load every summer. It is the Europe of the communion of saints. And this book is a gesture of gratitude.

—Olivier Clément

Dear Olivier Clément,

Seeing the faces of so many young people on our hill at Taizé, you have understood that they come here with vital questions: How can I find a meaning for my life? What is God expecting from me?

In Western societies, there are young people who are wounded in their depths by broken or torn affection. Sometimes their hearts are dying of solitude. And some of them, plunged into uncertainty about their future, are asking themselves: Does my life still have any meaning?

But it is also true that many young people are doing everything within their power to find a way out of the gradual spiritual collapse which is affecting the West. Faced with a crisis of confidence in humanity, these young people are thirsting to take on responsibilities so that trust can grow. Without that, how could human societies be built up?

It is a disintegration of spiritual values in many regions of the world that has stimulated our community to welcome young people week after week, not only from all parts of Europe, but also from Africa, Latin America, and Asia. And it is the same disintegration that leads us to go to live near young people from one end of Europe to the other and to question ourselves together with them.

Some of my brothers also live among the very poor, in the continents of the South. And it comes about that sharing the daily conditions of great poverty is a kindling breath of the Gospel. Even from very far away, this breath penetrates the vocation of those who are in Europe.

Dear Olivier Clément, you have a practiced intuition. You have grasped so well what my brothers and I would like to live out day after day. And you have understood it with your Orthodox soul, and that gives you the ability to see very far. I would like to express to you the confidence of my heart.

—Brother Roger of Taizé

1

A Meaning to Life

In search of meaning

What overwhelms me when I come to Taizé is to enter the enormous Church of Reconciliation and to see those thousands of faces, those thousands of different expressions.

Why is it that every year thousands upon thousands of young people from all the five continents keep arriving at Taizé in an uninterrupted pilgrimage, week after week?

Young people have an extraordinary thirst for the absolute. And it is sure that nowadays many of them make visits to monasteries. Why is this? Is it because they are looking for God? What they find in monasteries is above all a sense of mystery, of peace, and of depth, in fact of everything that is lacking in the societies where we live. I remember once meeting the great film director Tarkovski, who said: "The challenge for our age is to let humanity remain a question; to avoid thinking that everything is straightforward, that everything is explainable." It is very important that there should be people and places and actions which ask the question of the mystery of life, the mystery of God.

But it is not enough just to ask this question, because to ask it is to discover that an essential characteristic of humanity is incompleteness. And if humanity is incompleteness, if it is characterized by a lack of something, then it is also desire, for desire is both the awareness of such a lack and at the same time it is energy. So what is also necessary is to awaken a sense that there are answers to this question. And it is here that a witness becomes important, a witness like that of the Taizé Community—one which does not require any special knowledge to understand it, but which is made accessible to everyone. In this world, a world which is not so much bursting forth as collapsing in on itself for want of meaning, young people find at Taizé a response, a meaning to life.

First of all, they find people who are willing simply to listen to them, and this is something which they find extremely important. But on the other hand, they also come to Taizé because they want to be told certain things, and to experience certain things. They often come because it is their friends who tell them about the community, and at the present time, friendship is one of the most important ways for people to discover faith, since some young people really know nothing of the Christian message any more. I suppose there must be a sort of "legend" about Taizé, partly in France, but even more in other countries, and now increasingly in Eastern Europe. It is talked about as an extraordinary place, a place of international encounter, a place of prayer which goes beyond the normal possibilities. So people come to see, and in general they are struck by it: it is impossible to remain indifferent at Taizé.

In this place, there is the power of a prayer that is lived out in a very simple way. It is a sort of learning by practice for young people who have perhaps never prayed before—at least not consciously, for every human being prays in one way or another. The young person of today has a head which functions at full speed, either with ideas and systems, or else simply with desires and whims furnished by the media. But the spaces of the heart are left fallow. So in order to have the possibility of grasping this prayer that is in all of us, it becomes very important to pacify the intelligence. Words that are spoken too quickly or too soon become mere wordiness which joins the non-stop wordiness of our age. And that is why the time of silence experienced during the prayer at Taizé, and which the young people happily join in, is absolutely fundamental. In the silence, prayer is matured, and this allows the words of the prayer, when they start again, to be something different from the usual chattering. We are in a world where there is a sort of enormous verbal inflation; but at Taizé it is just the opposite, and that attracts people. The deep sense of mystery is rediscovered as a kind of "inner light," and the young people feel it. It radiates from a face, a face that allows us to interpret all other faces in this light; and this is a great miracle.

Not only do the young people coming to Taizé experience this depth of peace and silence; by way of contrast, they find that they are also in a place of encounter and festival. And the encounter and festival are just as authentic as the peace and silence. Their contact with the community allows them to discover an example and an inspiration rather than taboos and prohibitions. The meaning and the reasons for things are explained, and that changes everything. For there is no moralism at Taizé. What they find there is a community of people who are both very human and open, but at the same time live with great restraint in their relations. Human relations are not inhibited, but lived out in a way that allows them to stay within their proper limits, with a kind of reserve or modesty. And for these young people it is a prodigious example. This is something we need to take account of: they have a great thirst for modesty without knowing it, and in fact this modesty makes possible the development of the person. So this is something else that they are looking for at Taizé, something which is quite unconnected with moralizing, and which is very important.

Another thing which attracts them is without doubt a peaceful kind of beauty. They live in a world where art is sometimes violent, where music too can be violent, and where the body is exalted but is sometimes twisted and loses its significance. But at Taizé there is a different beauty; there is what Dionysius the *Areopagite* calls "the beauty of communion." He says in his treatise *The Divine Names* that beauty is a name of the Divine and that this beauty is the origin of all communion. But beauty as it is understood in present-day society is more often a beauty of frenzy and even of possession, with an element almost of magic. However, the young people find at Taizé a beauty that is calm, deep, and pacifying; they find it by means of songs that are both very beautiful and very simple, by means of icons, and by means of people's faces. For nothing is more beautiful than a face illuminated by an expression of trust and gentleness. And in beauty there is a mystery which is ultimately the mystery of God.

Finally, in a world which is becoming more and more compartmentalized and homogenized by collective hatreds, young people at Taizé enter into an experience of unity in diversity, and that answers once again to their deepest needs. In society there are compartments, but there is also a planetarization: people travel more and more from one end of the world to the other, and they have a real sense of the universal. But in a world which is becoming more and more unified, all sorts of stresses appear, innocuously called "problems of identity." That is to say, each person or group becomes somewhat afraid when faced by this unification which seems to be about to drown everything in the same technological greyness, and so they strongly assert their own identity; and in general they assert it in opposition to other people. But at Taizé young people are attracted because, while the sense of the universal is there, at the same time the identity of each person is preserved. Nobody is asked to renounce their nationality or church; on the contrary, by these differences people are expected to enrich each other and learn to accept each other; and so young Christians are able to experience unity in diversity. This is a truly incredible experience in the world as it is. At this point in history we need to go beyond both abstract universalism and particularisms that confine people and conflict with each other. And at Taizé there is a concrete universalism as well as particularisms which open in communication.

Unselfish listening opens onto mystery

In our society there is very little listening. People talk, but they only listen on condition that they get a chance to talk afterwards: it is like a succession of monologues. In this situation, to find someone who will listen to us, there is nothing left but to go to the psychiatrist!

Now we ought to see how to make the link between the search for the unconscious and the reality of the supraconscious which points towards meaning. For in the human unconscious there is not only the biological or cosmic subconscious, connected with the destiny of each person since their childhood (as Freud and Jung discovered), but there is also a supraconscious (as the "psychoanalyst of existence" Viktor Frankl realized) which desires meaning and which points towards mystery. Moreover, especially when the "forty years threshold" described by Jung is passed, but also beforehand, the source of neurosis is often to be found not in religion but in the absence of meaning, that is to say in the absence of religion in the deep sense of the word. One could say that in the depths of the heart, Christ is there waiting for us in order to give meaning to our existence. And so little by little, in the spiritual life, the heart will open up. And to open up is all that it asks. This is why it is so important that the young should be able to meet people who are quite simply people who welcome, precisely because they are set free by their goodness, by their prayer, by their restraint, and by their capacity to welcome in an unselfish way. It is rare to find love that is unselfish: love so often seeks gratification—one loves in order to be loved—or it is taken only in a carnal or even carnivorous sense. But for monks, there is this possibility of living out an unselfish love which opens onto the mystery of God and the mystery of the person, and it is probably this which attracts the young people most of all.

Moreover, we live in a society where there is undoutedly a crisis of fatherhood. Now, a monk is a paternal presence, even if he is very young (his age, in fact, does not matter at all). He is at a certain distance from the usual interplay of passions, and at the same time he offers a welcome. And this is something that young people are very aware of. They are in search of a spiritual fatherhood which can teach them how to live, and to find meaning; they are in search of people who can be like an incarnation of meaning and with whom they can speak from the depths of themselves about what preoccupies them. Young people need the presence of someone who does not demand anything and who is simply ready to listen. And the monk does not ask anything for himself; he does not seek to capture or absorb or seduce; and so he is ready to listen. So these brothers at Taizé, to whom they can open their hearts—and it is rare in our day to be able to speak of certain fundamental things—fulfill a ministry which is absolutely essential.

A power for life, creation, and love

At Taizé, there is no emphasis on sin. I am extremely happy about this, because young people who know nothing about Christianity often imagine Christians as people who tell them:

"You are sinners!" It is a theme of all the reactionaries of our age, to the point of obsession, to say that the young have no sense of sin any longer, but in fact that is not true at all.

There is an "innocence of being" that has been taken away from us by a certain kind of historical Christianity. This innocence of being must be rediscovered and given back to the young; we need to help them realize that the reality we call sin is not what they think it is, but that in fact it is a condition they already know from experience.

Sin is a mysterious separation. It is this feeling we sometimes have that we are so close to paradise in the beauty of the world, in the look of trust in someone's face, or in the wonder of love, but that this paradise, in spite of everything, is lost. For even a great love risks ending in a failure in which one is no longer of any value to the other, in which the look that gave me life turns to stone; or if it does not end like this, it can be cut short by death. We can walk in a countryside full of wonderful beauty and be filled with joy, but suddenly sadness appears, because we have the impression that this beautiful world has no personal awareness by which to welcome life: it is doomed to death. Paradise is near, and I cannot enter it. So maybe I try to trick my way into it, trying to enter it by means of drugs, for example. But it does not work. I end up losing my sanity or else I simply kill myself, and I am found dead of an overdose in an unknown street at the age of thirty. This is the condition of sin, and young people feel it profoundly. When someone speaks of solitude, of anguish, or of human distress, they understand very well what the condition called sin is. And it is also because of this that they come to Taizé.

This is why, when people say that the young have no sense of sin, I reply that it is not true and that young people are sick and tired of being preached at about the sins of the flesh. Talking about what is permitted and what is forbidden does not help.

25

Instead, we ought to be talking more about meaning. We need to speak positively. If we give the meaning of what we say and if we speak positively, it is possible to bring others little by little to change their life; but this will not work if they get the impression that Christianity is a set of rules or a kind of moralism. Christianity is not moralism: it is energy, it is fire! As Pasternak wrote in one of his novels: it is the point at which life reaches "its highest degree of intensity."

So it is important really to know how to understand young people both with their needs and with their creative energy. We need to understand their thirst for compassion and their disgust with the destruction of the environment and with the extraordinary inequality between East and West, between North and South, and to grasp their desire for universality. And so, little by little, we will be able to speak to them about the mystery of Christ and the mystery of the Holy Spirit as a power for life, for creation and for love which transfigures the condition of sin, coming as a response to human distress and anguish.

"I could only believe in a God who dances!" said Nietzsche.

But Christ is this "God who dances"! One can see this, for example, in the fresco of the Church of the Holy Savior at Chora, Constantinople: in this picture Christ descends into hell, breaking the doors of hell with one foot; and with the other foot he begins a movement of reascension in a shining whiteness, and he pulls up Adam and Eve out of their tombs. There he is, the "God who dances"!

And the Christian is the person who dances too, in the joy of knowing that love is stronger than death, in the joy of knowing that we are no longer blocked in a space-time that death has sealed up! There is no more death! There are places on the way of life that may be hard or may be sorrowful, but they always lead through towards the resurrection. This living Christianity is what young people discover at Taizé.

2

A Parable
of Communion

A communion made real

If I had to describe where the brothers of Taizé belong in the great family of those who have lived in community since the first centuries of the Church, I would say that their place is in both a great continuity and a great newness.

Life in community developed in the fourth century around Saint Basil in Asia Minor. At that time, the Roman Empire had been converted and the Church had subsequently split into two parts; on the one hand there were the monks who lived in solitude and who sought extraordinary experiences, and on the other hand there were the masses of people who had joined the Church out of mere conformity. Saint Basil wanted to make the link between the two by creating communities which would be simply gospel communities living in brotherly love, like the parishes of the primitive Church. This is how community life was born, and it seems to me that Taizé belongs in this tradition.

Life in community has always been to some extent a life of hospitality. But the newness of the hospitality at Taizé lies in the fact that it has grown to meet the needs of today. And in tune with the rapid changes of history in our time, this hospitality continues to create something new on the basis of three themes that have arisen out of each other: the theme of reconciliation among Christians, i.e. the ecumenical theme; the theme of evangelization, aimed at the crowds of young people from all over the world who sometimes know very little about the mystery of faith; and the theme of a Christianity that is creative.

Of course there are all sorts of monastic communities which practice hospitality, but it is not usual to find one which is in itself a communion of monks coming from different Christian denominations that have tragically wounded each other over the course of history. At Taizé there is a communion among Christians which is made real; and this is very new and very important.

From the linguistic point of view, there were once multi-lingual monasteries in the Christian East, which grew up around the men who revived the great tradition of the prayer of the heart, the Jesus prayer; but to rediscover this in the context of modern times, in Europe, is equally new.

So Taizé embodies both continuity and newness. And this is the way in which the Tradition of the Church ought to be understood, since the Tradition is the life of the Spirit in the Church. On the one hand, the Holy Spirit is the memory of the Church and the faculty of discernment within the Church; but on the other hand, the Spirit is equally the eschatological tension of the Church and is therefore also perpetual newness.

Separate from all and united to all

Traditionally, monks have been a leaven in the Church and in society. In fact, two conceptions of monasticism have emerged in history. Firstly, there has been the idea of a monasticism implanted at the heart of society. This conception means that even the hermit who lived in the desert became at a certain moment a spiritual father, and people came flocking to him. This was the case with Anthony the Great, at the beginnings, and it was even the case with the stylites who lived perched on high pillars in Syria in order to be left in complete tranquility, but who, at a certain point, agreed to come down from their pillar, to welcome people and to listen to them. Nevertheless, there has also been another concept of monasticism: the nostalgic idea of creating a perfect city, a city of the pure, living in complete separation from the life of the Church and of society. But this idea of a monasticism in isolation as a perfect society has little value for today.

More than ever, though, monasticism as a leaven is really indispensable. For example, in a country like Romania which preserved the Faith through the most difficult period, a few monasteries and certain spiritual figures offered hospitality to people by the hundreds. They kept no monastic enclosure, and it was in this way that the faith was able to remain very much alive for many people.

The life at Taizé seems to me very well illustrated by the words of a monk of the fourth century called Evagrius of Pontus: "The monk is separate from everyone and united to everyone." The Taizé community is "separate from everyone," because the brothers also have times of retreat, of distance, of silence and inner prayer; but they are "united to everyone" by their intercession and their hospitality. For the ministry chosen by the Taizé Community is in fact the presence of all these young people who come from everywhere, who search, who have a desire, and who have a thirst. There are enough brothers present during the liturgical celebration to form a kind of axis, as they kneel in a broad line down the middle of the church; if there were only three or four brothers, it would be different, but in fact there are more or less a hundred, and therefore they are not lost in the crowd and they can carry along the thousands of young people present. And then, they lead groups of young people in reading the Bible together, explaining it and sharing, or they simply stay available after the evening prayer to listen to them.

It is a form of monastic life which can come as a shock to some people, but it should not be a surprise: hospitality is a traditional value which has been adapted at Taizé to our own times, to our today and our tomorrow.

Let history be nourished by eternity

A society which has no monks, a society which is not in a way irrigated by monastic prayer, is a society that is really sick. We need places which are like laboratories where certain people devote themselves to this experience of depth and where the word "God" can be used without its being just a word but where it is really a presence of which one becomes more and more deeply aware. Through this, society comes alive. To illustrate this, I like to use the image of a snow-covered mountain: when the snow gradually begins to melt, what is happening has two sides. On the one hand the warmth, the blue of the heavens, is being concentrated in the snow and it blesses the mountain; and on the other hand the water is being drawn out and it forms streams and then rivers which allow gardens and fields to be watered, making life possible. Monasticism in society is like all this; it is immense, it is meaning, it is the blue of the heavens which is concentrated in the prayer of a few people who are dedicated to this inner experience and who, by touching young people, will diffuse this influence through the whole of society.

Thus what is happening at Taizé is altogether within the line of traditional monasticism. We must rediscover this function of the monastic life as a laboratory of eternity in order to let eternity nourish history. For if history is not nourished by eternity, it becomes mere zoology! This is what the brothers are called to; and from them the young people who come to them acquire the taste for it. Having discovered at Taizé a living Christianity, they in their turn will then try to become creators in every domain of life: in culture, in the economy, in politics and so on. Thus the life being lived at Taizé has a prophetic character; it is truly the twenty-first century that is getting under way.

A continual founding

It is now more than fifty years since Brother Roger founded the Taizé Community. In the history of monasticism, the periods of foundation have certain characteristic features both on the spiritual level and on the sociological level; and these same features can be seen in the development of Taizé.

Firstly, what I think we have at the beginnings of Taizé is a kind of vision, but one which is not a plan or a specific expectation. This vision is the vision of Brother Roger, and it was at first a vision of reconciliation among Christians and of service to people by Christians. But it was not a knowledge of what the future would bring, he did not expect what was going to happen and what is happening today. That is a fundamental fact. At the beginning there is an exceptional personality, and that personality draws people involuntarily. So we have this aspect of the unexpected and of involuntary attraction, and this is something which keeps appearing in the long history of monasticism. It is a law of the history of the Church: when something authentic is put into practice, people come. Those who sit down in their room to make plans, saying "I am going to found a community where thousands of young people will come" have already failed before they begin. Things do not come about in that way!

Another feature of this period of foundation is a growth that is rapid but organic. This growth comes about quickly, but it does not happen in a systematic manner. It happens in the same way that a seed gives birth to a plant, or as a plant grows—it always has a touch of the unexpected. For example, at one point at Taizé the numbers of people coming made it necessary to build the new Church of Reconciliation. At first, Brother Roger found it too large, but in the end the brothers needed to extend it; and so it continues.

A further sign that seems to me common to all new beginnings in monasticism is the movement from isolation to outreach. At the beginning, Brother Roger withdrew into a place lost in the depths of France, into Burgundy, a region that had been marked in the past with a spiritual imprint (it witnessed the age of Cluny, and that of Saint Bernard). But now Taizé is no longer isolated: it is a place whose influence spreads abroad and a place to which people congregate.

A final feature that seems important to me, and I will borrow a phrase of Saint Paul to express it, is that Taizé is "unknown and yet well known." It is clear that Taizé and Brother Roger are well known. But in the media, they are not well known in the same way as the stars, the sports heroes, the politicians or even the church leaders who make the headlines. Unknown and yet well known, because everyone has heard of Taizé and of Brother Roger.

Something that seems to me particularly interesting is that I cannot see how the foundation stage at Taizé could come to an end. I do not see how they will be able to say, "Now, that's it. Now it's founded." Why? Because we are in a period of history that is moving very quickly. We are not in an age of stability where something can be established to last for ever; we must constantly keep up with a history that is changing. Brother Roger has known how to do this in his own manner, without thinking it out in a systematic way. At a time which could be called "the heroic age of ecumenism" in a country like France, he started out from this concern for reconciliation—and it is still there—but today Taizé finds itself in the forefront of the new evangelization which John Paul II speaks of and which is becoming more and more clearly necessary. And tomorrow it will be something else again, perhaps a Christianity that creates culture and beauty with a prophetic dimension.

In any case, it would seem to me very difficult for Taizé to settle down. For with which of its founding intuitions could it come to rest? These founding intuitions are successive, but they are nevertheless all related: evangelization does not go against ecumenism, ecumenism and evangelization do not go against the idea of the creation of beauty or of a Christianity which is expressed through the culture of our age. All this continues, all this develops: it seems to me that Taizé is in a state of continually being founded.

Common life and reconciliation

The Taizé Community tries to make real a "parable of communion." The word "parable" in this expression introduces a certain humility in referring to their communion; the brothers do not claim that the community is an ecclesial communion that is fully realized, but that it is a question of a "parable." And what image of the Church is the Taizé Community called to be a parable of? It is that of a church brought together in diversity. This is the parable of Taizé: to show that the divided Church remains the One Church. People crucify the Body of Christ in trying to divide it, but still they are not able to divide it. For in its depths the Church is one, and this one Church is the undivided Church. We have a memory of and a hope for an undivided Church, but we also have the presence of the undivided Church, even in its very divisions. When we are called to experience these divisions, that is our cross; and at the same time it is a joy and a hope for us when we see witnesses to this profound unity. This unity is not something to be made: it is there to be discovered! And this is what is happening at Taizé, where there is a parable of the discovery of this unity.

The community brings together people with different denominational origins, who are living together because they are Christians. They want to be Christians together, both respecting their various backgrounds and leading a common life which is an example of reconciliation. The connection between the common life and reconciliation lies in the fact that the brothers of Taizé come from churches which have tragically wounded each other in the course of history, especially in the West since the sixteenth century. But by their common life they allow the undivided Church to become visible, not only as a memory of the early centuries but as a reality which is there and which needs to be discovered, through the holiness of one's brother or sister, and through the communion of saints who, for their part, do not allow themselves to be inhibited by the different Christian denominations. There is a communion of saints which unites the saints of North and South, of East and West. And all of this is present at Taizé. It is like a microcosm, with the presence of brothers from Protestant and Anglican backgrounds, of Catholics—and perhaps tomorrow of Orthodox brothers—from every kind of ethnic origin, speaking different languages, and gathering round them young people from every kind of background and of a huge variety of languages. It is the opposite of Babel: what we are witnessing at Taizé is an experience of Pentecost, and that means an experience of the undivided Church. The undivided Church is the Church of Pentecost. Up until now, we have been breaking the Church into pieces, while keeping the pieces quite homogenous. But now we need to put the pieces together, without making a cacophony, in this sort of Pentecost harmony which is being continually sketched out at Taizé, in a kind of evolution which is always renewed, which goes from one beginning to another.

What really matters is communion

For those who are tempted to separate truth from communion, it is important to remember that Christianity is not a system or an ideology. Christianity is Someone, it is Christ. And consequently, to be a Christian is to have a relationship with Christ, who is himself the truth. The whole idea of the truth needs to be re-examined, because we nearly always think of the truth as a system or as an ideology. Now, ideologies or words can clash, and that is not a very good approach to Christian truth. Here, we have to reverse our perspectives: dialogue can only be founded on this reality of communion. And communion cannot be separated from the truth; in fact it is itself the way into the heart of the truth, in the mystery of love, in the mystery of Christ and of the Spirit, in the mystery of the Trinity.

Christians really need to be told that if they enter into communion, they are experiencing the profoundest part of the Christian faith. The best and the most central part of the Christian faith is not a doctrine; it is this encounter, this love, this communion. And from this perspective, what might have appeared central often becomes peripheral and what might have appeared peripheral often becomes central.

Dogma has nearly always been formulated by a negative or apophatic approach; it has never claimed to articulate the mystery, but to safeguard our encounter with Christ. Among Christians it is extremely important to discover and to learn to love the other person's way of approaching Christ and of loving

Christ. There is no reason not to reach agreement in theology; a doctrinal question can never become completely stuck. People want to be doctrinaire because they are afraid. We are living at a time when people are uptight about identity, when each denomination is trying to assert itself in what is most specific to it; and denominations are seeking to define themselves by returning to the past, that is to say by thinking of themselves as being in opposition to something. This tendency needs to be combatted by an attitude which is both faithful and open, and by an awareness that in the end there is only one Church, a Church which we are wounding, a Church whose one, seamless garment we are tearing apart. The theological aspects are blown up out of proportion by the passions, and then everything comes to take place in the realm of passions and emotions. It is essential, then, for us to let the passions subside and to discover what really matters, that is, communion. We need to understand once and for all that communion is not a matter of sentiment, but that it is the most fundamental thing of all.

This is why at Taizé nobody makes speculations about ecumenism, but ecumenism itself is made real. The undivided Church is there, showing through; it is already experienced in the community by the existence of the community itself, and that is something that fills me with joy. At the same time, Taizé is still like an appeal, like a beginning, like a fresh start.

Many young people say that they "feel at home" when they find themselves at Taizé. And I must say that I too feel at home in this community which is preparing and anticipating the undivided Church.

3

Inner Life and
Human Solidarity

The mystery of Christ and the different religions

"Christ did not come to create one more religion, but to offer a communion of love to every human being." Language like this is often used at Taizé, and I think in fact that it is one of the tragedies of Christianity that it has become a religion just like the others.

From the religious point of view, humanity can be divided into two great hemispheres. There is the first, which seems to me to descend from the primitive religions, especially in India, in which everything is one, where in the end everything is submerged in unity. In these religions, the universe itself is holy, and everything is swallowed up in a kind of immense cosmic matrix like "dolls of salt in the sea," to use a characteristic image. And then there is the more "Semitic" hemisphere, represented by Judaism and Islam: God is in heaven and humankind is on the earth; they cannot truly enter into communion, but God gives his law, and humankind must follow this law, listening to the word of God. It seems to me then that Christianity is altogether astonishing, because it says that the human and the divine are united both "without separation" and "without confusion." (This was the affirmation of a great ecumenical council of the fourth century.) "Without separation"—this is the aspect emphasized by the spiritual hemisphere coming from India; and "without confusion"—the aspect affirmed by the hemisphere I have called "Semitic."

There is an extraordinary synthesis here. The mystery is that the God revealed by Christ is not in himself solitary; he is neither an ocean into which everything melts nor a solitary being in heaven, but he is the mystery of communion, that is, the mystery of love. He is the reality at the same time of the most complete unity and of the most complete distinction. And it is in this communion that humanity too is called to live, in this unity and this difference. Those who are united to Christ form a single being. They are not separate like solitary islands. But at the same time Christ meets each one of them in a unique way. The Biblical account of Pentecost reminds us that, when the Spirit descended on the gathering of the disciples, the flames were divided and rested on each one of them, consecrating each one in their absolute uniqueness, and opening an unlimited space for their creative freedom. This is why it is possible for the Christian to love the expressions of unity found in India, and also the mystery of the wholly transcendent God found in Judaism and Islam, while at the same time uniting the two. And this is something that seems to me quite incredible.

This always makes me think of an episode found in the memoirs of a missionary published in Moscow in 1917. This missionary tells how he found himself at a certain point among the Buddhists on the borders of Siberia and Mongolia. He ended up admiring them and loving them enormously. He admired the Buddhist lamas so much in fact that he said he did not have the courage to baptize them. Then, taking his reflection further, he added that the whole problem was how to open their eyes. For the eyes were there; but they were closed eyes, enclosed in their

inwardness, in that kind of purely inward fullness where everything is one. But if, he thought, while still preserving this power
of inwardness, they could open their eyes to see the other and to
love the other in his or her otherness, that would then be
Christianity, and it would be the very fullest kind of Christianity.
The whole question is here. It is a matter of leading those who
live enclosed in their interiority to open their eyes to see the
other, and of leading those who affirm the absolute transcendence of God to understand that, if God is so transcendent, he is
able to transcend even his own transcendence in order to come
to us, to become like one of us, to live with us, and to take us all
up in him; so much so that God in Christ takes on a human face
and allows us in the Holy Spirit to understand every human face
in God.

Incorporating the criticism of atheism
and the contribution of humanism

At the same time, Christianity needs to take on board the con-
tribution, the questioning, and the criticism coming from that
kind of modern atheism which is a destruction of idols. For
Christ is like a diamond with a thousand facets. He is the union
in fullness of all that is divine and all that is human, to such an
extent that all the explorations of the divine in all the religions
and all the explorations of the human in all kinds of humanism—including the humanisms that call themselves atheistic—
can reveal to us something of the mystery of Christ. We have to
live out Christianity as "divine-humanity," to use a term dear to
the Russian religious philosophers. And in this divine-humanity
there is a place for all the studies of humanity undertaken by
modern humanism and anti-humanism, in opening them onto

God; and there is a place for all the searching into the divine undertaken by all the wisdom and mysticism of the non-Christian religions, in opening them onto the human. All this should take place in this undivided Church which we are called to manifest, to reveal, and to uncover; for it is there, and it is already palpable at Taizé.

A mysticism that irrigates society and culture

In the West, the Christian faith is often identified with morals or with social or charitable involvement, while the spiritual experience, the mystical way that is its real heart, unfortunately remains unrecognized. Contemporary Christianity has been strongly influenced by a type of Marxist thought. I do not say this is altogether wrong, because I think that there are Marxist analyses that are extremely useful in the Third World. But Christians give the impression that they have gone off to the frontiers so much that they have forgotten the center, the heart. And while they have been away at the frontiers, invaders have arrived and have tried to take over the heart; and these invaders are the impersonal kinds of Asian mysticism.

Even more, we have so much tended to make God into a hoary old man with a beard and a little bird that pops up from under it that people do not want anything more to do with what they suppose is meant by a personal God. They would prefer the oceanic god of the New Age and of the mystics from the depths of Asia.

Although a kind of atheism based on indifference is very widespread, we are now moving more towards a mystical kind of atheism. All this was profoundly sensed by Dostoyevsky. In *The Devils* there is an extraordinary character for the future: Kirilov. Kirilov is a sort of mystical atheist. He expresses his attitude when he says: "Good and evil are the same for me. As for God, why bring him in? I look at an autumn leaf: it is there; it is green with a little yellow near the edges. Everything is beautiful, everything is well, I am experiencing a moment of eternity. I am going to kill myself in a moment of eternity, and then I will be God." This is what we are moving towards. But what we need is Kirilovs who are converted and healed: Christian Kirilovs. This is how Dostoyevsky was himself; when he suffered from epilepsy he had extraordinary experiences of illumination in one instant, but later on he understood that he had to come to grips with faithfulness, with the mystery of Christ who is not merely man but who is God-man. Dostoyevsky had a true awareness of how much today's society reveals the abysses and the fissures in humankind. But in the depths of these abysses he discovered Christ. He said that we must choose between the God made human, that is, Christ, and the humanity that wants to become God. This is the position we are in today, and much of the New Age current is humanity trying to become God.

So we need to rediscover some of the paths of the deepest kind of Christianity, to show that God is not an individual or three individuals in the sky, and to rediscover the sense of inwardness, the sense of mystery. We need to do a bit of "negative" theology, and allow ourselves to say that we cannot really speak about God because God is beyond all concepts and all images. So the living God can reveal himself in the mystery of Christ as the incarnate, crucified and risen God who raises us from the dead through an inner life. We need today to define a deep spirituality, a deep Christian mysticism which can at the same time irrigate society and culture. This is why a liturgy and a life of prayer like that experienced and transmitted at Taizé is so important.

Spiritual experience and creative opening to the world

I remember a young Japanese intellectual who came to Paris to write a thesis. His subject was Nicolas Berdyaev and the Russian intellectuals of the beginning of this century who had been followers of Marxism but who had finally changed their position. I asked him why he had chosen this theme, and he replied: "I used to be a Marxist too, but not any longer." We talked, and I asked him this question: "And has this led you to a deeper kind of Buddhism or Shintoism?" And he answered: "No, that does not interest me. What interests me is a Christianity like that of Berdyaev, a Christianity which allows one both to have a profound spiritual experience and to be open to the world in a creative manner."

This link between a deep spiritual experience and a creative opening to the world is at the heart of the meetings at Taizé, which have been centered for many years on the theme "inner life and human solidarity." This is the kind of Christianity we should be aiming at, for the more someone becomes a person of prayer the more they become a person who is responsible. Prayer does not set us free from the tasks of this world: it makes us even more responsible. In fact, nothing shows more responsibility than to pray. This is something which really needs to be understood and communicated to young people. Prayer is not a diversion. It is not a sort of drug for Sunday morning. It involves us in the mystery of the Father, and in the power of the Holy Spirit, around a Face that reveals every other face for us, and which in the end makes us servants of every human face.

Becoming servants of every human face can take the concrete form of being present with those who are suffering from being abandoned by others, or from poverty—as is the case, for example, with the twenty or so brothers of Taizé who live in deprived areas in other continents —, but it calls us as well to be inventive, to be creators in every sphere, including that of economics, that of a global civilization, of culture, and so on. Christianity must be creative, as in fact it has been enormously creative in history. To realize this, it is enough to look at the Romanesque churches in the villages of the European countryside, not to mention Notre Dame at Paris, or Rublev's icon of the Trinity! What a power of creation! And there is no need to have a label in order to create in this way. Dostoyevsky did not call himself a "Christian novelist." But he is one of those to have taken an extraordinary step forward in human sensibility, in thought, and, I would even add, in Christian theology. He has a huge number of readers at present. He is one of the "fathers" of modernity, quite as much as Freud, Nietzsche and, in the recent past, Marx. So it is up to Christians to begin this creativity again and to continue with it in the world as it is, without lamenting the past. The world does not need Christians who are whiners; it needs Christians who are creators!

4

Entering into Mystery

A *deep spiritual experience*

Our culture puts enormous value on the intelligence, on desire
and sexuality, and sometimes also on a kind of aggressiveness in
group expression; but we put much less value on the "heart," by
which I mean the most central part of the human being. People
today live mainly in these three dimensions: either the intellectual dimension; or that of aggressiveness and violence; or in the
dimension of desire, which is constantly being beaten into us by
the whole atmosphere of the age. So the problem is, how can we
make the intelligence descend, and how can we make the desire
rise up into the "heart"? This is important because the heart is
the crucible where they will find themselves purified in the fire
of grace and where the human being can truly become unified
and go beyond itself; it is the place where we can be unified within ourselves and opened up.

Now, Christianity has a whole tradition of repetitions which
can pacify us and which can, in a sense, empty the intellect of its
agitation and allow it to be united to the "heart." And this makes
us ready for prayer. For example, in the Eastern Church there is

what is known as the "Jesus prayer," or in the Latin Church there is the "Rosary."

Something very interesting at Taizé is that this formula of calming repetition has been taken up in the liturgy; that is, it is not used only in personal prayer, but also in prayer together or common prayer. Some young people, who know almost nothing of mystery, are introduced to it here, and they begin to learn how to pray. And this opens them onto the deepest part of themselves; it opens them onto the "heart" which is the center of integration and the place where the whole person opens up and goes beyond itself. Humanity discovers itself there, for, being in the image of God, we do not truly exist except when we are connected to God. So when these people pray for the first time, it is as if something is torn open. This is an experience which I have had myself. I grew up as an atheist and for many years I was totally ignorant of prayer, until I was almost thirty. I remember that when I prayed for the first time, it was like a sort of tearing open, as if all my opacity was being pulled apart and a spring of water that had been silted up suddenly began to flow, in the same way that when you dig and dig suddenly the water comes springing up.

This kind of prayer cannot be something too complicated; a very intricate style of singing (like that of the Benedictine monasteries in the West or of the great Byzantine tradition) would not work at Taizé, because the young people would not understand it. But what is offered to them at Taizé is the basic essentials in only a few words. And, in fact, the essentials in Christianity really can be expressed in a few words. So they sing a song and take it up, everyone in their own language, and it is extremely calming. A kind of gentleness comes with this repetitive singing, a sort of inner peace, and that is so important. I do not believe that this has been done very much in liturgical traditions before, but it has certainly been an important part of personal prayer. And since the young people often do not know what personal prayer is, and often do not know what liturgical prayer is either, it really is a good thing to be able to give them the essential realities in this form. In this way, it becomes possible for them to live out a deep spiritual experience.

A silence that is inhabited

Another thing that can contribute to the discovery and development of an inner life is to have times of silence. In our world, silence is generally something poor. Silence is empty; it is sad. And so people fill it up with noise. This may be noise inside us, thoughts which whirl around and around, associations of ideas, desires, and dreams; or else if it is not that, there is the radio, the television, channel surfing.... In fact, we are in a world of continual noise; we are busy with something all the time. And because of this it has become very important for us to learn how to become silent, and at the same time to let this silence become an inhabited silence. There are times of silence during the prayers at Taizé, which are preceded and followed by singing; and the result of this is that the singing can penetrate them so that the silence becomes prayer. And in that prayerful silence, the deep forces that exist in everyone but which are normally dormant begin to wake up. I have already said that in our civilization everything that has to do with the intelligence and sexuality is very well developed, but that the forces of the heart, the spaces of the heart, rest fallow. But at Taizé, it is precisely these forces of the heart which are awakened in this profound, this "full" silence.

Furthermore, all young people, I think, have an experience of God; only they do not realize it. They all have a feeling of mystery. This is something they have felt in the beauty of the world, in a work of art, while playing the guitar one evening, or in the coming to birth of love. They all have some such experience, and they need to be helped to discover that these experiences are not isolated or dislocated or meaningless, but that they are rooted in depth. What is to be avoided is the attempt to grasp hold of these experiences by means of drugs, for example. The person who takes drugs is a kind of Don Juan of these experiences, who wants to repeat them systematically. At Taizé, on the other hand, through a sort of discipline of silence, people are taught first of all how to listen. They are taught words that are not banal, not radio or television words, but words which are made to nourish the soul, and which will permeate their lives.

This approach to silence and this calming repetition are very important. Afterwards, little by little, it becomes possible to move on to reading longer texts and to singing more developed hymns; but first of all it is necessary to enter into mystery.

Awakening the spaces of the heart in everyday life

The mystics say that most of the time we are a bit like sleepwalkers: it is possible to accomplish a lot of things, to be someone of great integrity, to have a very full agenda, and yet all the time to be living like a sleepwalker, never able just to stop to admire something, to love, or simply to wonder. It is essential to learn how to wake up. There was a Byzantine mystic of the fourteenth century, a man called Nicolas Cabasilas, who was a layman who held high office at an appalling period when the Empire was in the throes of constant invasions and civil wars. He tried to say something to Christians who, like him, lived in the tumult of the world, and what he said amounts to this: "Know that Christ is in your heart, and that if you entrust yourself to Christ, your heart will be kept safe." Thus he urged people to take part in the liturgy of the Church in an intense way and, from time to time during the day, to make what he calls "brief meditations": "You are walking in the street and you are very busy, but suddenly you remember that God exists, that God loves you, and that Christ is present in the depths of your being. If you do this, little by little, your heart will wake up."

But not only should all of us try to open up the depths of the heart; we should also be trying to create cultures that are irrigated by this sensibility, for this is something that can be expressed also in art, music, paintings, poems, and so on. What we are doing when there is an intense liturgical life is creating an art form that comes straight from and speaks directly to the heart. It is not possible to create a culture linked to the mystery of the heart unless we first create a liturgy that expresses this mystery of the heart. And this liturgy will go hand in hand with an abundant creativity, beyond the walls of the Church, which will shatter the sleepwalking of humanity.

Knowing God with our senses pacified and transfigured

There is a very fine film by Bergman called *The Seventh Seal*, in which, after an exhausting march, a sort of wandering knight meets a group of bohemians on a clifftop beside the sea. A young woman gives him a bowl of milk to drink, and when he has finished it, he asks the question: "Is it so desperately impossible to know God with the senses?" For my part, I believe that this is just what the liturgy ought to do; it should enable us to know God with the senses, pacified and transfigured. The beauty of common prayer touches the senses and makes it possible for inwardness to be awakened.

We should set up a training program for priests and pastors to try to tell them that what can touch people most is a beautiful and simple celebration of the liturgy. Some of them sometimes have the impression that on the contrary, it is all over, and that people do not want that any more; but this is a very great mistake. People need to rediscover the power of the liturgy. And in the West there is a real need to regain the sense of mystery in the parishes.

The most fundamental thing that the liturgy ought to transmit is the mystery of the resurrection, that is, the mystery of life that is stronger than death, the fact that the love of Christ is conqueror of death and hell. This should happen in such a real way that when someone leaves a church carrying in them this power of life, they can truly recognize that every person they meet has a face, and that the whole world is a gift and a message from God.

A liturgy ought to help us understand all this little by little, and it is good thing if it does not go too fast or say too much. At Taizé the liturgy expresses the beginning of many things; it is a liturgy that awakens many things. And since most of the young people there come for a whole week, the brothers can already go further during the last three days: every Friday, Saturday and Sunday take on their full liturgical significance. Friday is always Good Friday, Saturday is the Great Saturday with the mystery of Christ's descent into hell and into death, and Sunday is always Easter. During these three days the liturgy becomes more ample, and it becomes a true expression of the mystery of life stronger than death.

5

An Inrush of Light, Peace and Love

God is never the author of evil

"God is never the author of evil. He wants neither suffering nor human distress. God does not want wars, nor earthquakes, nor the violence of natural disasters. He never arouses fear or anguish, but he shares the pain of those who pass through incomprehensible trials." These words of Brother Roger can often be heard in the Church of Reconciliation. And they answer to a question that nearly all young people find themselves asking sooner or later, a question something like this: "If God exists and if he loves us, why is the world so evil? Why are so many things in the world ugly, spoilt, rotten, or lost? And why is there not only a chaotic sort of evil, but also a perverse kind of evil, evil that seems to be in a way designed to make us doubt?"

There really are powers of darkness which give evil its perverse character, and which cause God to be more and more forgotten or sometimes even feared. We cannot avoid sensing in this evil a will that wants to make us doubt. This is what is known as "original sin" in the symbolic story in Genesis. In this story, the woman and the man began by calling into question the goodness of God; they thought that God was a tyrant who monstrously forbade them to eat from the tree of life. But in fact all the while this idea was something being insinuated to them by the serpent. And they ended up by doubting the love that God had for them.

The argument against faith, continually trotted out more or less consciously, goes like this: "Look how terrible the world is! If there was, as you say there is, an all-powerful God of love, the world would not be so dreadful." This was the argument of Ivan Karamazov in Dostoyevsky's novel: "How could I agree to the existence of a world that was perfectly organized and designed if it was necessary to pay for it all by the torture of one little child? I refuse such a world and I return my ticket to God." We are in a society where people use this argument to return their tickets to God and to deny his existence.

It is really necessary to say to young people that God is not "all-powerful" in the sense that this concept spontaneously suggests to us. Certainly, only an unlimited power could have created other free wills. With our human limitations, we can only create reflections and images; we cannot create another person. God, however, has created others, but in doing so he has also given them space for their freedom, because love cannot use force. The Fathers of the Church, and in particular the Greek Fathers, expressed it like this: "God can do everything except compel people to love." So it is true that God is almighty, but yet his omnipotence is fulfilled in total weakness; he allows others to exist in their freedom, a freedom which can turn towards good as much as towards evil. This is a mysterious, basic fact. God cannot do anything in the world except through hearts that open freely to him; but when hearts do open in this way, he acts like an inrush of light, of peace, and of love. He can never act from the outside, like a dictator or like a hurricane. Nicolas Berdyaev even went so far as to say that "God has less power than a policeman."

If we start with the idea of an omnipotence that does every-thing, that means that God causes his creation to be both won-derful and spoiled; and that way of thinking does not hold water! But if we start by saying: what is wonderful is what God is accom-plishing, and what is spoiled is that evil which is trying to ruin God's work, then we can situate ourselves in this combat.

"Where is God, then," said Ivan Karamazov again, "when a child is hunted and eaten by dogs?" Well, God is precisely in that little child who suffers and who dies! This is the same experience as the one related by Elie Wiesel; he was in a prison camp, and one night he stood in front of a body on the gallows, and asked himself: "Where is God?" And he suddenly had this intuition: God is the man who was hanged. This is the mystery of the cru-cified God as Christ has revealed him.

Breaking the spiral of evil

I have always liked this reflection by François Mauriac: "If you meet someone who explains to you the very origin of evil, send him to me and I will strangle him!" The important thing is not to speculate about evil, but to break this spiral of evil in which, thinking that the world is bad, people end up thinking that God does not exist; and the more people tell themselves that God does not exist, the worse the world becomes. It is a terrible spi-ral, and it must be broken by means of this openness of heart which allows God to enter the creation: if men and women open themselves freely to God, then the divine energies (energies of goodness, of love and of true creative power) will be able to spring forth in the world.

Whoever is the most excluded, whoever is the most forgot-ten, whoever is the most misunderstood, this is God. He looks and asks if there are any hearts that freely let go of themselves and open themselves to him. For if he can enter the world through them, the world will change. This is the reason for the importance of monasticism, for monks are people who open up sources, so to speak, from which this inrush of light, of peace and love can flow.

A mystery of communion

To let this inrush of light, of peace and love flow out is the very vocation of the Church. At Taizé it is often recalled that the Church is a "mystery of communion." And this "mystery of communion" is first and foremost the mystery of the Trinity. God is communion; he is one, and he is also in himself the mystery of the other, so that there is in God the pulsation of love. And in the same way, human beings, because they are made in the image of God, are called to find fulfilment in a free communion. We can make a beginning of this in Christ and in his Church. And so the Church is a communion, and it is even the communion par excellence; that is to say, it is this diversity which is respected, and at the same time it is this unity in Christ. However, the indicative becomes an imperative: the Church *is* communion, and it must also *become* communion, for sometimes it falls away from it. And it is for us to remember that every time this happens, every time we find the Church falling away from its calling to be communion, we need to "dig deeper." If we "dig deeper" we find, not nothingness, but the risen Christ who raises us from the dead; not nothingness, but this immensity, this ocean of love, this "ocean of light," as the Syrian mystics say. This is not an ocean of light in the Hindu sense, but an ocean of light that radiates a Face. Communion is given, communion exists in depth, because Christ is there in depth.

An intimacy without limits

At Taizé, through the common prayer and through the meetings offered every day, young people from all over the world live out an experience of communion. Now, to try humbly to live out experiences of communion—of which perhaps the simplest, within the Church itself, is the experience of friendship—is really fundamental. Patriarch Athenagoras of Constantinople insisted on this very much: "Jesus did not love people in an abstract or general manner. Before his passion, he went to see Martha, Mary, and Lazarus. So he had friends, and therefore he had preferences." That worried the Patriarch for a moment, and then he said to me: "Yes, that is to say that Christ prefers each person." Each person is preferred by Christ; each face is lit up by a flame of the Holy Spirit. This is a great mystery that is difficult to express. Christ is our intimacy without limits; that is, he is not only an individual and emotional intimacy, but also an intimacy which opens outwards, an immense intimacy in which we are not separated from anyone, from the origin of the world until its end, across time and across the continents. All human friendship, all human communion, is never more than a very humble interpretation of this total unity which we receive in Christ. Every time we interpret a little this infinite mass of love that carries us, every time we find in friendship an experience of communion through moments of shared silence or of encounter in depth, we are experiencing the reality of the Church.

In the West, people who pray

The brothers of Taizé have never wanted to create a movement centered on the community. On the contrary, far from keeping the young people for themselves, they stimulate them to be bearers of peace, of reconciliation and of trust in their towns, their universities, their places of work and their parishes. This unselfish welcome is something absolutely fundamental for the young people. I would like to underline how important this is for the young Orthodox Christians who come to Taizé. It needs to be understood that the Orthodox Church is, because of its history, a Church which is terribly bruised, a Church which has suffered much. And this suffering has often come about at the hands of the West and of Western Christianity in its aspect as a dominating power, that is to say in its non-Christian aspect. This is why Orthodoxy has been led to turn in on itself; and it has had difficulty in escaping from this withdrawal, this complex of both inferiority and superiority with respect to the West.

It is very important that Orthodox Christians should go to Taizé. There they feel welcomed, respected, and loved; there they find a Western world which does not seek to conquer them or to convert them—as has so often been the case in history. They find a Western world which does not consider itself superior to them, but which expects something from their testimony. And their testimony is extremely important for everyone. But at the same time they will be able to discover that the others are Christians, too, and that there is a profound Christian life in the West, a mysterious communion of saints which goes before us.

At Taizé there is this immense possibility of opening them up, of showing them that in the West there are people who pray and who are searching at the same sources as themselves—that is, the Scriptures and the Fathers of the Church—and this is something which is truly interesting and striking for them. We need to understand that there has been a centuries-long heritage, augmented by the Communist domination, which crushed some extraordinary buds of openness. At the beginning of the century,

Russia had fully taken her place in the reality of Europe: she had become a European nation among the other European nations, something which did not stop her from being Russian and Orthodox, or from contributing to European culture while remaining Russian and Orthodox. And then there was the crushing experience of seventy years, with a bullied church, withdrawn into itself, living essentially by its liturgy, and feeling everything outside itself as hostile. So, to discover at Taizé that the others are Christian brothers and sisters and that a reconciliation is possible is the service that the community can render to young Orthodox Christians, and I believe it is immense.

In the midst of a secularized society, rediscovering what is essential and letting it nourish us

In the past, something that weighed heavily on Christianity was the desire for power, that is, the desire to show itself right by strength, and the link with the state. And so a new question comes up: what role are Christians called to play within society now that it has become secularized?

What the Church now has to do is to give up all claims to power, but it must do so without ceasing at the same time to be a leaven, and it must continue to be a leaven in every sphere. Free from all power, the Church will be able to have an illuminating influence that will be more or less discreet, or more or less apparent according to the time, the place, and the possibilities of history.

It is also necessary for the Church to give up the idea of having an exterior influence on society. It can only have an influence from within, through minds and hearts that are enlightened, and through all sorts of initiatives that are going to spring up from them. The role of Christians is not to struggle against the secularization which is now a fact of life. It is rather to make this secularization into something positive, that is, to make it into something which will allow the Church to be a ferment and not a power, and which will also allow it to ask ultimate questions, questions about the ultimate meaning of existence, to which secularization has no answer. Perhaps God is expecting from Christians a creative spirituality which can enable them to modify gradually, by osmosis, the foundations of culture and society.

All this is very important, for, at this moment in time, we have been freed from a kind of Christianity that is seen as the ideology of a community, a nation, or a state. We are free of the inquisitions and from the need to have great influence or an important position. Today, perhaps for the first time in history, Christians are becoming poor and free. There is an openness in what is small, in simplicity; new realizations are coming about; there is a return to the essentials. And it is this joy of rediscovering the essentials, and of living out the essentials, in a Church which is personally and consciously wanted by its members, that is the great advantage of our age. And it is in this joy and this confidence that the meetings of young people at Taizé take place.

6

From Anguish to Trust

Trust will have the last word

One of the key words at Taizé is "trust." The meetings organized by the community in Europe and on the other continents make up part of what is called a "pilgrimage of trust on earth." The word "trust" is perhaps one of the humblest of words, one of the most everyday and simple words that there are, but nevertheless it is one of the most essential. Instead of speaking about "love," of agape, or even of "communion," of koinonia, which are heavy words, we could perhaps more often speak of "trust," because in trust all of these realities are present. In trust there is the mystery of love, the mystery of communion, and finally there is the mystery of God as Trinity.

It is to the extent that we carry within us the anguish of death, or the fascination with nothingness that leads ultimately to murder and suicide, that we are lacking in trust. Now, we are all in fact encompassed in the mystery of the resurrection, because Christ encompasses all of us in his humanity. It has often been forgotten that Christ's humanity, as well as being personal, is at the same time universal. But this is a theme that is very clear in the best Christian theology; in the Greek Fathers, for example. When they say that Christ takes on human nature, they mean that he takes all humanity into himself. There is no human being who is left outside Christ; Christ is united to every human being, and every human being has their place in the mystery of the resurrection. Only, there are people who know this—the Christians—and who give thanks for it, and there are people who do not know it yet.

So, if we start from this mystery, deep within us, in the crucible of the heart, the anguish of death will gradually come to be replaced by the certainty of the resurrection, and by the joy of the resurrection. From then on, we no longer have the temptation to project our anguish onto other people, or to make others into scapegoats for our anguish or into objects of enslavement. We can love our neighbor, and we can be full of trust and radiate trust, because we know that we will never die, and that we can say to our neighbor: "You will never die. You are risen in Christ. You are risen in the power of the Holy Spirit."

To show trust does not mean ceasing to be lucid. As Christ says, we must be both "as shrewd as snakes" and "as innocent as doves". If we have trust within us, we do so in a lucid fashion, knowing that we may have to go through an experience of the cross, an experience of death, but that, because Christ is risen, this experience of death will not have the last word. Yes, we can trust, even as we go through the most difficult moments, because we know that in spite of appearances, the resurrection is going to have the last word, and that therefore trust will have the last word.

The human person in its very being is love

The parable of the good Samaritan, in which the Samaritan is the "other" in the most negative sense of the term, ends with an astonishing reversal. The question put to Jesus at the beginning was: "Who is my neighbor?" But at the end he asks this quite different question: "Who is the one who acted as a neighbor to the wounded man?" He does not say: "Which one considered the wounded man to be his neighbor?", but: "Which one considered himself to be the neighbor of the wounded man?" So this capacity to go towards others is something that we carry in ourselves; and perhaps our trust will meet with the other person's own deep desire to enter into the mystery of communion as well. For the human person in its very being is communion; in its very being it is love. Only, we do not know it; it is something obscured, masked, or diverted. And moreover it is the very strength of this love—but of love when it has become perverted and lost its ultimate goal—which can make separation into something so strong.

So we can be lucid, clearly aware of difficulties and problems, but all the while we can face them in trust, that is, in faith, knowing that in humanity there is this deep desire to be communion, to be love, and so to be trust.

Rediscovering a "joy of being"

Together with trust goes the spirit of childhood. By this I mean an attitude that has nothing to do with childishness but which consists first of all in knowing that we are not orphans. Our contemporaries very often suppose that they are orphans: there is this endless universe, these galaxies, these black holes; we are descended from monkeys and we are going towards nothingness. Christ, however, reminds us firmly that we have a Father, and we can have confidence in him. And then the spirit of childhood opens onto a "joy of being". And this joy of being is something we are called to rediscover in God.

Certainly some people will ask how it is possible to rejoice, considering that there are such trials in human life, and that others are suffering from war, from torture, or from hunger. But in the face of all kinds of suffering, this joy of being expresses itself in the form of compassion. This is an experience that we often have. Suppose we have heard something that gives us great joy, some good news, for example; perhaps someone we love has pulled through after a serious danger. We are carrying in us a great joy, but that great joy is not going to make us insensitive to the suffering of other people. On the contrary, it can make us even more sensitive, and we will be able both to carry this great joy within us and to enter profoundly into the distress and suffering of our neighbor at the same time. There is no contradiction; joy is not opposed to compassion; I would even go so far as to say that joy nourishes compassion: it is because we have the joy of the risen Christ deep within us that we can enter fully into love and compassion. To see an opposition between them is false and meaningless.

We must be open to sadness while at the same time bearing joy within us. This is possible because we know that ultimately the resurrection will have the last word, and that ultimately the last word is on the side of joy. We know that even in the earthly history of a human life, the empirical reality is not all there is to be said: destinies continue, the Kingdom is coming. And consequently it is possible for us to bear joy, sadness, and distress within ourselves all at the same time. It is a matter of transforming the cry of horror before the bronze wall of destiny (as in Greek tragedy) into the cry of Job; and in doing so we shall come to understand one day that God himself became Job, and has opened up for all the Jobs of history the paths of the resurrection, which are ultimately the paths of joy.

We must be witnesses to joy. If we are not, then humanity will be drowned, either in sadness because of death, or else in absurd paroxysms where we strive to forget it: eroticism, drugs, and all other forms of oblivion. So we need people and communities like Taizé, who bear witness to joy. This is something essential, for such a witness can transform sadness because of death into sadness offered to God; and thus the creative attitudes which will reduce the evil in the world will be possible, although we know that we will always have to struggle against stupidity, against wickedness, and against all forms of evil, until the end of time. But struggle we must, and this is possible because we carry joy in ourselves; it is joy that gives us the strength to struggle.

And above all, no one should feel any sense of guilt because they are joyful. Once again, joy is not opposed to compassion, but nourishes it. Joy is the bringer of life.

At the core of things, not nothingness but love

The reality of trust and joy is renewed in prayer. Saint Paul calls us to "rejoice without ceasing" (Philippians 4,4), but he adds also that this means confiding one's worries and anxieties to God through prayer (Philippians 4,6). In another of his letters, he even tells us to "pray without ceasing" (1 Thessalonians 5,17). But how can we pray without ceasing?

This is a question that people have been asking since the very first days of Christianity. A Church Father like Origen, in his *Treatise on Prayer*, said that to pray without ceasing is to feel that one is not isolated or abandoned. For we are tempted to live our lives in a sort of cocoon or tunnel, bricked up with our problems, our worries and our anxieties. Now, what is being asked of us is to break out of this interior tunnel, to tear it open. This can be done in various ways, for example by the invocation of the name of Jesus, as in Orthodox spirituality, by a cry to God for help, or by a Taizé song and so on. At the beginning of the nineteenth century, Saint Nicodemus the Hagiorite suggested using the prayer: "Jesus, Jesus, my beloved God!" This interior tunnel can also be broken by the "brief meditations" which Nicolas Cabasilas spoke about in the fourteenth century and which we have already mentioned: I remind myself that God exists and that he loves me.

And when we find ourselves unable to pray, there is still the possibility of offering to God our incapacity: "I cannot pray, but I offer you my inability. You, you are my prayer." For we need to understand as well that our prayer is not just a matter of our prayer to Jesus, but that it is also the prayer of Jesus, which he is constantly offering to his Father. So if we really cannot pray—and this is something that can happen—it is always possible to give this inability to him, and to do that is to pray without ceasing, too.

To share with God our wonder and admiration, or our worry, anguish or suffering gives us every time the sense that we are not lost. It makes us aware that at the core of things there is not nothingness, but love. And in the end, this is what it means to pray without ceasing: to live with this inner conviction that at the core of things there is not nothingness, but love.

7

Love Offered to All

God gives his love to everyone

At Taizé, one is completely liberated from the caricature of God as someone who causes fear, a God who condemns, a God who induces guilt. Such a caricature is a terrible thing, and it separates many young people from the mystery of God. But Saint John writes: "God is love" (1 John 4,8 and 16). It is not possible to go beyond this; in these words, everything has been said.

One of the most terrifying things in the history of Christianity has been the conception of hell as a sort of eternal concentration camp created by God for those who do not want him. It is as if God had an attitude like this: "Ah! You do not know me! Well then, I do not know you either!" Saint Isaac the Syrian, a great mystic of the seventh century, is perhaps the person who has written the deepest meditations on death and hell. He was Bishop of Nineveh, and, almost blind, he ended his life as a monk, plunged in prayer. He said: "How can we imagine that God should create hell, that God should create a place of distress, of torture, and of abandonment? All God can do is give his love. He gives and will give his love to everyone: he will be all in all."

77

There are several steps in his meditation, which go something like this: The first step is that all God can do is give his love. The second step goes on to say that this love can be humbly welcomed by people and become in them an infinite joy. This is what is called "paradise." However, God's love can also be refused by people who close themselves against it. Such people clench themselves up inside, and upon all the suffering that they have been able to provoke; for the human being has the ultimate liberty to do this, and it is precisely this that is the mystery of what is known as "hell." The fire of hell is in fact nothing other than the love of God, but it is the love of God when it is rejected and felt as something scorching. Then finally, the last step of his meditation consists in saying that God is not "just" in the human sense of the word "justice." And he cites all the parables in the Gospels, beginning with that of the workers who arrived at the eleventh hour, where it is made clear that the justice of God is not a human justice, but that it is love. And so, it is possible for us to pray that everyone may be saved.

God is stronger than evil

We should not suppose that God is less sensitive than we are to the evil committed by humanity. On the contrary, it is in fact God who suffers from it the most. The difference is that with God, evil never has the last word! God is stronger than evil! Here we can see the whole power of the Christian faith: there are no strong people and weak ones, there is no division into people with integrity and people without; there is only Christ, who is everywhere. He is the one who descended into hell, and he keeps on descending into our inner hell. And therefore we are never lost, even if it sometimes feels as if we are. Yes, it is true that when we come into the light of God we discover our whole life with lucidity, and we find that every tear that we have been the cause of can become an inner hell for us; but it is also at that moment that Christ appears and that he puts himself for ever between hell and us: "This hell I have taken on myself. And so, what I give you is the love of the Father and nothing else."

Saint Theresa of Lisieux once said: "If I had committed all possible crimes, I would feel that this multitude of offenses was like a drop of water in a burning brazier." And in the writings of Isaac the Syrian, there are pages of great beauty which culminate in a song of praise to this savior God who gathers us all in his love, who takes us all up in his love.

A hope for everyone

"God wants all people to be saved" (1 Timothy 2,4). What sin means—but it is never a final sin—is to fail to understand the full impact of the resurrection, to fail to understand the full power of the resurrection to save all people. Sin in the last analysis is despair. Someone has said that the sin of Judas was not to betray Christ, but to despair of his own salvation. And even there I am not really sure: when we talk about Judas, what we are denouncing is the Judas within each one of us. As for the person of Judas, all we can do is to commit him to the mystery of God, since, after all, the purpose of prayer is not to make God merciful, but to open people to the mercy of God.

And we must pray for everyone, because universal salvation is not something automatic. Yes, in the heart of God, everyone is saved, but it is still necessary for people to open themselves to the salvation that is offered to them. Now in prayer, life and love circulate, and to put a human being into relation with God, with his mercy and his light, by praying for them always makes a difference. Only, this difference is something that we have no possibility of measuring, for God is not limited by space or time, and a human existence as well extends to the infinite.

I remember once meeting a great contemporary mystic, Father Sophrony of Mount Athos. I asked him what would happen if a human being refused to open their heart and welcome the love which was offered to them, and this is the answer he gave: "Be sure," he said, "that as long as there is someone in hell, Christ will be there with them." And in the same tradition, all those who have written commentaries on Isaac the Syrian have reminded us that God stays at the door of every heart, even the hearts that remain closed to him, and that, if necessary, he will wait for all eternity until they open to him.

This hope for everyone is something I have found again at Taizé. For it is a community where there is a true awareness that all God can do is give his love, and that Christians are called to do the same, that is, to be bearers of this immense joy of the resurrection, and to pray that every human being may accept this love that is offered to all.

Historical Note on Taizé

Everything began in a great solitude when, in August 1940, at the age of twenty-five, Brother Roger left Switzerland, the country of his birth, to go and live in France, where his mother came from. For several years, he had felt the call to create a community which would make real every day reconciliation between Christians, "where kindness of heart would be lived out very concretely, and where love would be at the heart of everything." He wanted this creation to begin in the distress of the time, and so as the Second World War was raging he settled in the little village of Taizé, Burgundy, a few miles from the demarcation line that cut France in two. He hid refugees, notably Jews, who knew that in escaping the occupied zone, they would find refuge in his house.

Later, others came to join him as brothers, and it was on Easter Day 1949 that the first seven brothers committed themselves for their whole life to celibacy, to common life, and to a great simplicity of life.

In the silence of a long retreat, during the winter of 1952-1953, the founder of the community wrote the Rule of Taizé, expressing for his brothers "the essentials that make common life possible."

Starting in the fifties, some brothers went to live in disadvantaged places to be with people who were suffering.

From the end of the fifties, the number of young people coming to Taizé began to grow substantially. From 1962, brothers and young people sent by Taizé began to come and go continually in the countries of Eastern Europe, with great discretion, in order not to compromise the people they were supporting.

In 1966 the Sisters of Saint Andrew, an international

Catholic community founded seven centuries ago, came to live in the next village and began to take on some of the tasks involved in welcoming people.

The community of Taizé today is composed of about a hundred brothers, Catholics and from various Protestant backgrounds, coming from more than twenty-five nations. By its very existence, it is a concrete sign of reconciliation between divided Christians and separated peoples.

The brothers do not accept any gifts or donations, nor do they accept their own personal inheritances for themselves, but give them to the very poor. They earn their living and share with others only by their own work.

There are also small groups of brothers in poor areas in Asia, Africa, and South America. The brothers there try to share the living conditions of those who surround them, striving to be a presence of love among the very poor, street children, prisoners, the dying, and those who are wounded in their depths by broken affection, by being abandoned.

Coming from the whole world, young adults arrive at Taizé every week of the year for meetings which can bring together from Sunday to Sunday up to six thousand people representing more than seventy nations.

Over the years, hundreds of thousands of young people have come to Taizé, to reflect on the theme "inner life and human solidarity." At the wellsprings of faith, they seek to discover a meaning for their life and prepare themselves to take on responsibilities in the places where they live.

Church leaders also come to Taizé, and the community has welcomed Pope John Paul II, three Archbishops of Canterbury, Orthodox metropolitans, the fourteen Lutheran bishops of Sweden, and numerous pastors from all over the world.

To support the young generations, the Taizé Community has launched a "pilgimage of trust on earth." This pilgimage does not organize participants into a movement centered on the community, but stimulates them to be bearers of peace, of reconciliation and of trust in their towns, their universities, the places where they work, and in their parishes, in communion with all the generations. As a stage in this "pilgrimage of trust on earth," a five-day European meeting at the end of each year brings several tens of thousands of young people to a city in eastern or western Europe.

At the time of the European meeting, Brother Roger publishes a yearly letter, translated into more than fifty languages, which is taken up and meditated on throughout the following year at the meetings at Taizé and those held in other parts of the world. The founder of Taizé has often written this letter in a place of poverty in which he went to live for a time (Calcutta, Chile, Haiti, Ethiopia, the Philippines, South Africa...).

Today, throughout the whole world, the name of Taizé evokes peace, reconciliation, communion, and the expectation of a springtime of the Church: "When the Church listens, heals, reconciles, it becomes what it is at its most luminous: the clear reflection of a love" (Brother Roger).